HEADSTART I

Religion and Irreligion in Victorian England: How Secular was the Working Class?

by

Hugh McLeod

HEADSTART HISTORY

Published by	HEADSTART HISTORY PO Box 41, Bangor, Gwynedd, LL57 1SB
Set by	C.B.S. 155 Hamilton Road, Felixstowe, Suffolk, IP11 7DR
Printed by	Henry Ling Ltd., The Dorset Press Dorchester
ISBN	1 873041 56 X

A CIP catalogue record for this book is available from the British Library.

CONTENTS

INTRODUCTION

The HEADSTART HISTORY PAPERS aim to identify themes and topics the significance of which extends beyond the studies of professional historians. The papers are distillations of the research of distinguished historians in a form appropriate to students and to the general reader.

This paper examines the historiography of working class religion, looks at the evidence and considers the various interpretations. It sounds a simple formula! It is, of course, a vast subject and the diversity of interpretation results from dependence on different sources and often, uncritical use of information available.

Ethnic groups, class structure, regional diversity and gender all contribute to the sources.

The role of the historian is interpretation and this complex period has produced two outstanding scholars who have contributed to the series. **David Bebbington's Victorian Nonconformity** has already established a strong readership and now Hugh McLeod of the University of Birmingham offers this important paper. He has written and lectured extensively on the subject and his new major work on poverty and piety in Berlin, London and New York will enhance our knowledge still further.

I add my thanks to Dr. McLeod for his contribution to the series.

Judith Loades
Bangor 1993

I

'No-one will ever understand Victorian England,' wrote the historian R.C.K. Ensor in 1936, 'who does not appreciate that among highly civilised, in contradistinction to more primitive, countries it was one of the most religious the world has ever known.'[1] This was the orthodoxy which prevailed until around 1960. Historians debated as to whether this religiosity was a good or a bad thing; they discussed when and why it went into decline; but no-one doubted that it was a reality. And indeed continental visitors who described their journeys across the Channel in the mid-Victorian years would have been of one mind with Ensor. The French writer, Hippolyte Taine, who visited Britain in 1858 and 1862, noted the packed churches and commented favourably on the high quality of the clergy - though he was not so keen on the British Sunday. As late as 1905, a guide to Berlin compared the irreligion of the German capital with the piety of London.[2]

The challenge to this consensus came from an Anglican bishop, E.R. Wickham, and an Australian historian, K.S. Inglis.[3] Wickham had directed the Church of Eng-

---

1 R.C.K. Ensor, *England 1870-1914* (Oxford 1936), p 137.

2 Hippolyte Taine, *Notes on England* (English translation, London 1957), pp 11, 158; *Berlin und die Berliner. Dinge, Sitten, Winke* (Karlsruhe 1905), pp 374-5.

3 E.R. Wickham, *Church and People in an Industrial City* (London 1957); K.S. Inglis, *Churches and the Working Classes in Victorian England* (London 1963)

land's Sheffield Industrial Mission. His concern with the lack of involvement in the church by working-class people in the years after World War II led him to trace the roots of this apparent indifference back to the nineteenth century and beyond. Inglis's interest was in Christian evangelistic and social reform movements of the later nineteenth century - ranging from the Salvation Army to the Settlements, to various forms of Christian Socialism. Inglis concluded that there was a common thread running through all these movements: they were a response to a general working-class alienation from the churches. Wickham and Inglis did not deny that the Victorian period witnessed what Wickham called 'a religious boom' - but they insisted that it was an overwhelmingly middle-class phenomenon, which passed the working-class majority of the population by.

They were able to challenge existing assumptions about the nature of Victorian religion, because of their rediscovery of two largely neglected sources: the censuses of church attendance conducted nationally by the government, and locally by newspapers at various points, notably the 1880s; and the numerous books, pamphlets and sermons by Victorian churchmen which deplored examples of working-class irreligion and suggested ways of combatting it. For instance Wickham quoted an open letter to Sir Robert Peel, published in 1840 by the Rev John Livesey of St Philip's, Sheffield, on the need for more churches and clergy in large towns. Referring to the low church attendance in his own parish of 24,000 people, Livesey commented:

> The wealthier classes, in tolerable numbers,

> are found occupying the pews; but the free seats are too often thinly tenanted. To what shall we attribute this indifference to Divine ordinances? ...The prevailing reason, I am assured, is the *force of inveterate habit*...they tread in the steps of their fathers, and are neither impressed with the obligation, nor feel the desire, of obtaining religious instruction. ...*The moral condition of the people is precisely what might be anticipated.* ...Can it be surprising that the profane doctrines and licentious practices of the Socialists, so congenial to the animal appetites of the ignorant, find numerous abettors? It is quite natural that in such a population, the demagogue and political firebrand will find abundant materials for sedition, treason and rebellion.(4)

Livesey's open letter was part of a large body of clerical literature, which often depicted working-class ignorance, infidelity and vice in lurid colours. In this case, as in many others, one may suspect that the picture was overdrawn for the benefit of the intended audience of politicians, businessmen and landowners, who had to be persuaded to channel money in the church's direction. However, it greatly strengthened the case argued by Wickham and Inglis that they were also able to cite 'hard' statistical evidence of working-class non-church-going. Especially important was Inglis's pioneering study of

---

4 Wickham, op.cit., p 87.

the national religious census of 1851.[5] In this he showed that average levels of church attendance were significantly higher in rural areas of England than in large towns. (Probably slightly under half the adult population attended in villages and small towns, whereas about a third did so in large towns, which were defined as those with populations of 20,000 and over.) He went on to argue that the main reason for the difference lay in non-attendance by working-class people, especially in London and the industrial north. In most of these places Nonconformity (especially Methodism) did better than the Church of England, but, according to Inglis, none of the churches made a significant impact on the urban working class.

The studies by Wickham and Inglis established a new historical orthodoxy. In the 1960s and '70s a series of local studies and thematic articles appeared which reached similar conclusions: the great majority of Victorian working-class people were indifferent, if not hostile, to organised religion, and the many attempts by Victorian Christians to convert the working class were a massive failure.[6] Some interesting new evidence was adduced

---

5 K.S. Inglis, 'Patterns of Religious Worship in 1851,' *Journal of Ecclesiastical History*, 11 (1960), pp 74-86.

6 Standish Meacham, 'The Church in the Victorian City,' *Victorian Studies*, 11 (1968), pp 359-378; Henry Pelling, *Popular Politics and Society in late Victorian Britain* (London 1968). More nuanced versions of this argument are presented in the contributions by David Mole ('Challenge to the Church: Birmingham 1815-65') and John Kent ('Feelings and Festivals', to H.J. Dyos and M. Wolff (eds.), *The Victorian City*, 2 vols. (London 1971).

to support this general thesis: for instance, Brian Harrison studied campaigns by Victorian Christians against drinking and cruel sports, and in favour of sabbatarianism, and argued that by attacking popular leisure patterns, these campaigns did a lot to generate popular dislike of the churches and chapels.(7)

Wickham and Inglis might be termed the leaders of the first generation of historians of Victorian working-class religion. They laid the foundations on which all subsequent researchers have built. The basic point which they established was the central importance of class in any discussion of Victorian religion. By the 1970s a second generation was emerging. They could take the work of the pioneers as given, and they now wanted to explore more deeply in one direction or another. The 1970s were a boom period for social history and for 'history from below'. Both these trends influenced the interpretation of working-class religion. Many historians began to ask themselves whether too narrow a definition of religion was being used. The idea that 'You can be a good Christian without ever going to church' is certainly widespread in England to-day, and similar views were commonly held in Victorian times too: was too much emphasis being placed on church-going as the measure of Victorian working-class religiosity? One of the major developments in this period was a growing interest in popular religion, the term used by Obelkevich in his seminal study of religion in rural Lincolnshire to describe a wide range of beliefs which were religious, but

---

7 Brian Harrison, 'Religion and Recreation in Victorian England,' *Past and Present*, 38 (1967), pp 98-125.

which diverged from the official orthodoxies of church and chapel.[8] Some of these involved the re-interpretation of the church's sacraments and festivals; some reflected a supernaturalism which had little or no connection with Christianity - as, for instance, in the important role of 'wise men' in the rural community, and in the widespread belief in witchcraft. Ainsworth's study of religion and politics in Lancashire suggested that working-class people who seldom went to church or chapel nonetheless believed in God and an after-life and were strongly committed to Christian ethics; he went on to argue that the specific form of socialism which emerged in Lancashire in the late nineteenth century was strongly influenced by local religious traditions.[9]

The other major development in the 1970s was the attempt to relate religious changes more closely to economic and social changes. The most widely-read study was that by Alan Gilbert, who suggested that in the long run industrialisation led to secularisation, but in the short run it helped to trigger a temporary religious revival. He argued that the great growth of Methodism, and of other forms of Nonconformist religion was a product of the early industrial period, and especially of the industrial village, where Methodism won a huge following among artisans, weavers, miners, and similar occupational groups.

---

8 James Obelkevich, *Religion in Rural Society: South Lindsey 1825-1875* (Oxford 1976).

9 A.J. Ainsworth, 'Religion in the Working Class Community, and the Evolution of Socialism in Late Victorian Lancashire: A Case of Working Class Consciousness,' *Histoire Sociale*, 10 (1977), pp 354-80.

The chapel offered community and emotional security at a time of social upheaval, and provided a religious legitimation for the denial of deference to social 'superiors.' But, according to Gilbert, the revival was running out of steam by the 1840s. Nonconformity was weakened by the revival of Anglicanism in the wake of the church reforms of the 1830s and '40s; but more important were the signs of incipient secularisation. Religious organisations failed to establish themselves as effectively in the emerging conurbations as they had done in the industrial village; technological progress destroyed some of the occupational groups most deeply involved in the evangelical movements of the early nineteenth century; above all, Gilbert argued that industrialisation was ultimately subversive of all forms of religion, because increased human control over the environment has provided technical means of solving most of the problems that formerly required supernatural assistance.(10) Stephen Yeo, in his highly detailed study of Reading, also tried to show that each stage of industrialisation had its own religious history, but the chronology which he suggested was rather different. He contrasted the mid-Victorian prosperity of Reading's churches and chapel with their decline in the period around 1900, and he argued that it was not industrialisation or urbanisation as such which undermined organised religion, but the specific form of capitalism that was emerging in the early twentieth century.(11)

---

10 A.D. Gilbert, *Religion and Society in Industrial England: Church, Chapel and Social Change 1740-1914* (London 1976).

11 Stephen Yeo, *Religion and Voluntary Organisations in Crisis* (London 1976).

One other important trend in the 1970s was the growing interest in oral history. In particular, two major projects, those conducted by Paul Thompson and Thea Vigne at the University of Essex, and by Elizabeth Roberts at the University of Lancaster, provided a wealth of information about religious beliefs and practices in the period from about 1890 onwards.[12] The potential importance of oral history for the study of working-class religion became apparent in the 1980s, and I shall return to this subject later.

With the 1980s, a third generation of historians emerged, many of whom have been much more critical of the Wickham/Inglis orthodoxy. The most influential book of this period was a study by the American historian, Jeffrey Cox, of the south London borough of Lambeth.[13] Cox accepted that working-class attendance at church and chapel was low; but in many other respects he challenged existing assumptions. Perhaps the most important aspect of his book was the discussion of the wide-ranging social role of the Victorian churches. At least until the early twentieth century, the churches had a crucial role in such fields as charity, education, recreation and politics: they thus entered into people's lives at many points, and could exercise a pervasive influence even in

---

12 For details, see Paul Thompson, *The Edwardians* (London 1975); Elizabeth Roberts, *A Woman's Place* (Oxford 1984); Hugh McLeod, 'New Perspectives on Victorian Working Class Religion: The Oral Evidence,' *Oral History* 14 (1986), pp 31-49.

13 Jeffrey Cox, *English Churches in a Secular Society: Lambeth 1870-1930* (Oxford 1982).

communities where church-attendance was low. His chronology and his preconceptions followed Yeo, rather than Gilbert: like Yeo, Cox stressed that the churches and chapels were in a flourishing condition for most of the nineteenth century; Cox also explicitly repudiated Gilbert''s determinism - the decline of the English churches in the early twentieth century was not the inevitable consequence of industrialisation and urbanisation, but a result of the specific ways in which they had chosen to respond to these developments. In the last few years, some younger historians have taken Cox's revisionism much further. Recent research has even questioned the assumption that working-class church-going was very low. Callum Brown in a provocative article entitled 'Did Urbanization Secularize Britain?' outlined a new synthesis which rejected the Inglis/Wickham orthodoxy at just about every point: big towns were not significantly less church-going than small towns; working-class participation in church life was much higher than has been generally assumed; the nineteenth century was a period of religious growth, rather than decline; when decline did come, it was associated with *suburbanisation* rather than *urbanisation*.(14)

I shall note in passing that at least four rival chronologies of Victorian working-class religion have been proposed. Some historians, such as Inglis, contend that the

---

14 Callum Brown, 'Did Urbanization Secularize Britain?' *Urban History Yearbook* (1988), pp 1-14. See also Jeremy Morris, 'Church and People Thirty-Three Years On: A Historical Critique,' *Theology*, 94 (1991), pp 92-101, a brief polemical essay which reaches similar conclusions.

level of working-class religious involvement was consistently low. A second view, favoured by Wickham, suggests that the level was generally low, but that there was some increase in working-class involvement in the period of relative prosperity between about 1850 and 1880. A similar chronology is suggested by Joyce, who stresses the influence in the mid-Victorian period of paternalistic family-firms, especially in the north-western textile districts, where many mills were closely linked with a particular place of worship.(15) A third view, argued by Gilbert, sees religious involvement reaching a peak in the turbulent and disease-ridden 1830s and '40s, and declining as living standards improved.(16) A fourth view, argued by such historians as Callum Brown, suggests that the peak came much later - perhaps as late as the 1890s.(17) These latter historians tend to take a relatively positive view of the achievements of Christian evangelists and social reformers; for instance, Alan Bartlett takes seriously Archbishop Lang's claim that the period from about the 1890s to the First World War marked the 'golden age of parochial work in the cities of England', and he also takes quite a favourable view of such other characteristic initiatives of this period as the Methodist Central Missions.(18) The evidence is at present inconclusive, a

---

15 Wickham, op.cit., p 131; Patrick Joyce, *Work, Society and Politics* (Brighton 1980).

16 Gilbert, op.cit., pp 112-114, 138.

17 Brown, op.cit., p 12

18 Alan Bennett Bartlett, 'The Churches in Bermondsey 1880-1939,' (University of Birmingham Ph.D. thesis 1987).

major problem being that though certain denominations (notably the Methodists), have good and easily accessible statistics, others (notably the Anglicans) do not.[19] The statistical trends may soon become much clearer.[20] But questions concerning changes in the nature of popular religious belief, or in the extent of the churches, social and political influence, will be much less easily resolved.

It will be apparent that rival theories as to *when* working class religion declined are linked to rival theories as to *why* it declined. One view - hinted at by several historians, but never worked out in detail - would be that the absence from church of the urban labourer was merely a continuation of habits formed in the countryside, and that the hierarchical nature of English society led to a general alienation from the church of those at the bottom, whether in town or countryside. For instance, Clive Field in a study of the diocese of Oxford over two centuries, showed that complaints by the Anglican clergy of irregular church attendance by the rural poor go back at

---

19 For a useful summary of Victorian religious statistics, see Gilbert, op.cit., pp 23-48, and for more detailed figures, Robert Currie, Alan Gilbert and Lee Horsley, *Churches and Church-Goers: Patterns of Church Growth in the British Isles since 1700* (Oxford 1977).

20 Robin Gill is conducting a comprehensive survey of church attendance statistics for nineteenth- and twentieth-century England. For some preliminary results, see his *Competing Convictions* (London 1989) and his contribution to Steve Bruce (ed.), *Religion and Modernization* (Oxford 1992).

least to the mid-eighteenth century.[21] Inglis, Wickham and Gilbert, however, emphasised the effects of industrialisation and urbanisation. Joyce detected a growth of working-class secularism towards the end of the nineteenth century, and linked it with growing class-consciousness and political organisation.[22] Recent research has tended to highlight the decline of middle-class religiosity from about 1890, and its consequences for other sections of the population.[23] It is beyond the scope of the present paper to assess the relative value of these theories. My own view would be that each of these types of arguments has at least some validity, and that an adequate explanation is to be sought through analysing the interaction of a complex mix of different kinds of factor, rather than through trying to identify a single key.

The remainder of this paper will be in three parts. In the

---

21 Clive Field, 'Long-term Trends in Religious Practice; The Diocese of Oxford 1738-1936,' forthcoming in *Southern History*. See also Gerald Parsons, 'A Question of Meaning: Religion and Working-Class Life,' Gerald Parsons (ed.), *Religion in Victorian Britain*, 4 vols. (Manchester 1988), 2, pp 70-72; David M. Thompson, 'The Churches and Society in Nineteenth-Century England: A Rural Perspective,' D. Baker (ed.), *Popular Belief and Practice*, Studies in Church History 8 (Cambridge 1972), p 270.

22 Joyce, op.cit., p 337. For a general interpretation of the connection between the rise of the socialist movement and secularisation, see Eric Hobsbawm's essay, 'Religion and the Rise of Socialism' in his collection, *Worlds of Labour* (London 1984), pp 33-48.

23 Cox, op.cit., J.N. Morris, 'Religion and Urban Change in Victorian England: A Case-study of the Borough of Croydon, 1840-1914,' (University of Oxford Ph.D. thesis 1985).

first, I shall discuss the evidence in support of a secular interpretation of Victorian working-class life; in the second, I shall explain why many historians have questioned this interpretation; and in the third I shall attempt to sum up.

II

Those historians who have stressed the secularity of the Victorian working class have a star witness in the shape of Horace Mann, the Anglican barrister who wrote the official report on the national religious census of 1851. Mann's report emphasised that a large section of the population was absent from church, and that the absentees were mainly drawn from the working class, which had become 'thoroughly estranged from our religious institutions'[24]. Not only were the working class not church-goers: they were, according to Mann, 'unconscious Secularists - engrossed by the demands, the trials or the pleasures of the passing hour, and ignorant or careless of a future'; and he argued that absence from church was 'attributable mainly to a genuine repugnance to religion itself'. He went on to analyse the causes of this estrangement, and he suggested six factors:

(1) The social inequalities within the churches - for instance, the system of hierarchically ar-

---

24 'Religious Worship (England & Wales),' *Parliamentary Papers*, 1852-3, vol 89, pp clviii-clxii.

ranged rented pews.

(2) The fact that class divisions in society ran so deep, that even if there were no such symbols of inequality within the churches, working class people would not wish to worship with members of other classes.

(3) The apparent lack of interest on the part of the Churches in the material well-being of the poor.

(4) Suspicion of the clergy, who were accused of making a business out of religion.

(5) The effects of poverty: many working-class people lacked time or space for reflection, and were too preoccupied with immediate problems to give much thought to religion.

(6) Lack of 'aggressive' missionary activity.

The last of these points is questionable. The later eighteenth and early nineteenth centuries were the golden age of the open-air preacher. Methodists led the way in a vast effort to bring evangelical Christianity to every village and hamlet of the land, and to every neglected court and alley of the cities.[25] In the 1830s and 40s, urban evangelicals went one step further, founding missions which specialised in going door to door, or pub to pub, bringing the message even to those who refused to listen

---

25 See, for instance, Julia Stewart Werner, *The Primitive Methodist Connexion: Its Background and early History* (Madison 1984); Deryck Lovegrove, *Established Church, Sectarian People* (Cambridge 1988).

when it was preached in public places.[26] Much of this work was counter-productive, as people understandably objected to being harangued on their doorsteps. But the Christians of this time cannot be accused of lack of energy in their efforts to reach the unconverted.

However, the other points made by Mann clearly have at least some substance in them. One dramatic episode may be taken to illustrate Mann's argument in particularly vivid style. In August 1839, the Chartists of Sheffield informed the vicar that they were going to attend the parish church as a body the following Sunday, and that they would like to hear a sermon on James V, 1-6: 'Go to now, ye rich men, and weep and howl for your miseries which shall come upon you...'. A newspaper reported that a large crowd of Chartists filled the church 'to the exclusion of a majority of the respectable seat-holders', but that the clergyman chose a text from Proverbs XXIV, 'My son, fear thou the Lord and the king, and meddle not with those that are given to change'. On a subsequent Sunday a fight broke out during the service, as a seat-holder tried unsuccessfully to oust the Chartists from his pew for which he had paid £6 a year. The vicar then applied to the magistrates for a police guard on the church, and on the following Sunday the Chartists arrived to find a contingent of police, armed with cutlasses, and with instructions to ensure that only 'decently dressed individuals' entered the church.[27]

---

26 Donald M. Lewis, *Lighten their Darkness: The Evangelical Mission to Working-Class London 1828-1860* (Westport, Conn. 1986).

27 Wickham, op.cit., pp 99-101.

During the 1830s and '40s class tensions were more acute, and the Church of England more unambiguously identified with the dominant classes, than at any time since. So it is unlikely that we would find many such dramatic confrontations in the latter part of the nineteenth century. However many smaller clashes took place, whether because of political differences between working-class radicals and the clergy or, more commonly, because working-class people felt that they were not treated as equals within the churches and chapels. As late as the 1920s, a working-class boy in Lancaster was excluded from an Anglican choir for wearing clogs - as a result of which his family broke with the church.[28] Robert Tressell's famous novel, *The Ragged Trousered Philanthropists*, published posthumously in 1914, provides a persuasive portrait of working-class life in Hastings, in which the churches and chapels make frequent appearances, but in a very largely negative role. The hero, a socialist decorator called Owen, is an atheist, who sees organised religion as a part of the machinery for keeping the working class in ignorance and subjection. Most of his workmates have some kind of vague religious belief, but in practice they see religion as largely irrelevant, and they are suspicious of the clergy - as one of them says 'As for all this religious business, it's just a money-making dodge. It's the parson's trade, just the same as painting is ours, only there's no work attached to it, and the pay's a bloody sight better than ours is.'[29] One of

---

28 Hugh McLeod, 'New Perspectives,' p 41.

29 RRobert Tressell, *The Ragged Trousered Philanthropists* (London 1955) [first published 1914], p 153.

the decorators *is* a chapel-goer, but he is ridiculed by his workmates, and he eventually turns out to be a crook.

Moreover, throughout this period, the severe poverty suffered by a large section of the working class had far-reaching effects on all areas of their lives, including religion. The well-known study by Charles Booth of London in the years 1886-9 suggested that 31% of the metropolitan population was living 'in poverty'; Seebohm Rowntree in 1898 suggested a figure of 27% for York.[30] Clearly other towns would have produced higher or lower figures, and there were also variations over time: for instance the figures would no doubt have been higher in such a period of deep depression as the years 1839-42, and lower in a very prosperous period, such as the early 1870s. But throughout the Victorian period there was a substantial section of the working class living in dire poverty, and another large section of those living on very tight budgets.

Extreme poverty tended to exclude organised religion - or indeed any other kind of organisation - except in so far as poor people might attend church in the hope of receiving money or free meals. It was partly a matter of lack of money for subscriptions; partly shame at being unable to wear 'decent' clothes; partly a preoccupation with the business of scraping a living. A missionary who went door to door in a poor area of Birmingham in 1838 referred to a poor woman who used to attend a

---

30 Charles Booth, *Life and Labour of the People in London*, 17 vols. (London 1902-3); B.S. Rowntree, *Poverty: A Study of Town Life* (London 1901).

Methodist class, but was excluded when she failed to pay her class money, and her husband who had attended a Baptist adult school, but gave up when he had to pawn his clothes. He summed up the response to his message in this impoverished district by saying that : 'The anxieties of the present life so incessantly occupy and fill the mind that [preaching the gospel] is like putting more in that which is already full.'[31] Furthermore, some of those who suffered poverty felt a sense of bitterness against God. According to a London working-class autobiographer, writing in 1911:

> Our attitude to religion was - that somewhere in the skies there was a God, the Father of the human race, and the Maker of the World. To certain favoured individuals He was kind, and provided good food and raiment in return for a regular attendance at church. The people in our own street, especially our own family, had been overlooked by God, and it was foolish to expect deliverance from our troubles by any other source than our own abilities. Thus we felt sure that there was a God, but that He was no friend of ours, that it was no use to depend on Him for anything, and that it behoved us to sharpen our wits and fight the

---

31 Diary of Joseph Derrington, 26 January 1838, Carrs Lane MSS (Birmingham Reference Library). For fuller discussion of these diaries, see Geoffrey Robson, 'The Failures of Success: Working-Class Evangelists in early nineteenth-century Birmingham,' Derek Baker (ed.), *Religious Motivation*, Studies in Church History 15 (Oxford 1978), pp 381-391.

> world for what we could get.[32]

For many working-class women, non-involvement in the church was not so much a deliberate choice, as an inevitable part of a way of life that was overwhelmingly concentrated on home and kitchen. Cooking and washing for a large family, keeping the home clean, and maybe eking out their husbands' meagre wages by some form of homework, left little time or energy for anything else. For many such women, their only daily relaxation was gossiping with neighbours or relatives, and their only treat was a Bank Holiday outing or a big family occasion. In interviews with oral historians, the refrain 'She couldn't: she hadn't the time' greets all questions about any life the interviewee's mother might have had outside the home. For one London woman, for instance, who combined bringing up a family with work in a factory, the one respite was provided by the death of workmates: the employer would allow a holiday with pay, so that everyone could attend the funeral, and afterwards the women from the factory would go on a big drinking spree before returning to the grind the following day. A London man brought up in a poor family in the early years of this century, remarked that his father's main objective, when he had finished work, was to get away from the house, but 'the mother with children was handcuffed. No emancipation at all, no.'[33]

---

32 George Acorn, *One of the Multitude* (London 1911), pp 50-51.

33 Interviews on Family Life and Work Experience before 1918 (Department of Sociology, University of Essex), no 261, p 32; no 245, p 10.

There were also many ways in which the humiliating social distinctions prevalent in contemporary society could find their way into the church. The best known example was the system of hierarchical seating operating in many churches and chapels. Victorian places of worship generally employed a system of seat-rents, by which individuals or families paid a quarterly rent for the use of a particular seat or pew which was then reserved for them. If the rent were sufficiently low, or if there were little differentiation between the amounts paid for different seats this did not necessarily cause internal dissension. Simon Green has shown that in 1870 every congregation in Halifax and Keighley charged seat-rents, including some strongly working-class Methodist and Baptist chapels. In one such Wesleyan chapel the most expensive pews were 1s3d a quarter and the cheapest were 9d, so the differential was tiny. On the other hand, in another, more prestigious, Halifax Wesleyan chapel the range was from 18s to 2s a quarter.(34) Many places of worship had a clearly defined hierarchy, with highly-rented seats at the front, and low-rented and free seats in galleries, or behind pillars.(35) As one Chartist critic put it, most churches and chapels had

> no place for the poor. They had no clothing fit for such select companies, and if they ventured there in such as they had they were thrust

---

34 Simon Green, 'The Death of Pew Rents, The Rise of Bazaars, and the End of the Traditional Political Economy of Voluntary Religious Organisations: The Case of the West Riding of Yorkshire, c.1870-1914,' *Northern History*, 27 (1991), pp 198-235.

35 Wickham, op.cit., p 78, Appendix 3.

> into great pens in obscure corners called ''poor seats'' and thus publicly advertised to the very respectable people present as paupers.[36]

Relations between the clergy and their working-class parishioners could also be difficult. This problem was most acute in the Church of England: Anglican clergymen were gentlemen; of those ordained around the middle of the century, about 70% had taken degrees at Oxford and Cambridge Universities, though in the later part of the century the proportion dropped to around 60%[37]; they spoke and dressed in ways that set them apart, and they often lived in large, comfortable vicarages.[38] In the various branches of Nonconformity, the situation was more complicated, because of variations between and within denominations. The proportion of middle-class ministers tended to be highest among the Congregationalists, and probably the Unitarians, and lowest among the Primitive Methodists, with Baptists and other branches of Methodism some where in between. The long-term trend was towards an increase in the proportion of ministers who were university-educated, or who at least had a formal training.[39]

---

36 Eileen Yeo, 'Christianity in Chartist Struggle 1838-1842,' *Past & Present*, 91 (1981), p 132.

37 Alan Haig, *The Victorian Clergy* (London 1984), p 32.

38 There is a good discussion of the relationship between Anglican clergy and their working-class parishioners in Bartlett, op.cit., pp 119-129.

39 See Kenneth D. Brown, *A Social History of the Nonconformist Ministry in England and Wales 1800-1930* (Oxford 1988).

Victorian churchmen were well aware of the barriers erected by class, and in their attempts to present Christianity in a form that was attractive to working-class people they attempted many experiments. Perhaps the most famous was the Salvation Army. The Salvationist uniform was classless; they went into the streets to reach out to those who never entered a church building; they used music to draw a crowd; and when they had got a crowd, they preached a simple and forthright message, with no doctrinal complexities.[(40)] The numerous mission-halls which filled the back-streets of Victorian cities used some of the same ideas: their shed-like buildings were felt to be less intimidating than the Gothic arches and stained glass windows of the conventional church or chapel, and the fact that these halls were directed specifically at the poorer working class meant that lack of 'decent' clothes might not inhibit poorer people from coming.[(41)] These churches of the poor did sometimes attract considerable numbers. In particular, the Salvation Army, founded in the later 1870s, grew spectacularly in the 1880s, reaching about 100,000 members

---

40 The definitive history of the Salvation Army has yet to be written. Inglis, op.cit., provides a good introduction. The official history is R. Sandall and A. Wiggins, *The History of the Salvation Army*, 5 vols. (London 1947-68). The best study of the Army's religious context is John Kent, *Holding the Fort* (London 1978). Glenn Horridge, 'The Salvation Army in England 1865-1900,' (University of London Ph.D thesis 1989), is a pioneering study of the Army's social composition.

41 Mission Halls have been largely neglected by historians, but there are useful discussions in Bartlett, op.cit., pp 286-294, and Cox, op.cit., pp 136-142.

by 1900.[42] Yet so far as the majority of the working class was concerned, the puritanical life-style demanded by the Salvation Army may have created as big a barrier as the class divisions within more conventional churches. Salvation Army soldiers were barred from drinking, and officers were barred from drinking or smoking. In their hostility to drink, the Salvationists were only taking to more extreme lengths a taboo that was already well-established in the other branches of Nonconformity;[43] but in thus making teetotalism a condition of membership, they were defining it as the supreme test of practical Christianity in a way which even other Nonconformists might have deemed a bit extreme.

Drink was a central part of the institutions established by working-class men, which provided a major alternative to the churches and chapels. In clearest contrast to the latter were the pubs and working men's clubs. The rivalry between church and pub was well stated by the son of a Nottingham hosiery worker: 'There was nothing else to do, only church or chapel or public houses, that was about all there was, and if you went to church or chapel you was a snob, and if you went in a pub you was a hail fellow well met.'[44] Here is how Charles Booth described the attitude to the church of working men in the East End of London in the 1890s:

---

42 Gilbert, op.cit., p 42.

43 See Brian Harrison, *Drink and the Victorians* (London 1971); Ian Sellars, *Nineteenth-Century Nonconformity* (London 1977), pp 40-45.

44 McLeod, 'New Perspectives,' p 36.

> They like their club with its pot of beer, its entertainments, its game of cards or billiards, or the 'pub' and its associates and a bet on tomorrow's race, but they look on these things as inconsistent with a religious profession, and every form of religious association thus becomes (if they think seriously about the matter at all) something from which in honesty, they must hold themselves aloof. They are unwilling to accept a restraint that would deprive them of these everyday pleasures, and the step to denounce as hypocrites those members of religious bodies who live mundane lives is thus easily made. ...Coupled with this there is some class feeling against joining churches which are supposed to side with the rich, so that to go to church may even be regarded as disloyalty to class. Thus there springs up a public opinion amongst themselves which in their workshops may make a favourite, if not a hero of the man who most defies religious restraints; who is even most reckless in his life and conversation.[45]

Among occasional pub-goers there were many who also went to church. But night-in, night-out pub-going seems to have excluded regular church-going to a greater degree than anything else. The important factor seems to have been the degree to which the drinker was integrated into a pub-based sub-culture. Pub and church were competitors for the worker's free time; but they also nour-

---

45 Booth, op.cit., 3rd series, 1, pp 85-90.

ished opposing sub-cultures. While the one brought men and women together, and stressed the virtues of family life, the other tended to offer the attractions of an all-male environment; the one offered easy-going good fellowship, while the other encouraged an attitude of purposive self-improvement; the one tolerated or encouraged activities that were tabooed by the other, including gambling,[(46)] poaching, swearing and 'broad' humour. Of course there were many people who emotionally had a foot in both camps, like the Darlington labourer, who spent every night in the pub, and never went to mass himself, but ensured that his children did, taught them their prayers, and brought them up to revere the Catholic Sisters; or like miners' leader A.J. Cook's father, who, as a keen drinking man, felt that he would not be welcome in the chapel, but liked his daughter to read him religious books. But the interviews conducted by Thompson and Vigne with survivors of the Victorian and Edwardian years make it clear how far pub and church were alternatives. Taking interviews with those brought up in working-class families in the industrial districts of northern England and south Wales, we find that 33% of non-church-going fathers were reported to spend most of their free time in the pub, and 25% of the fathers who were occasional church-goers, but only 7% of those who were regular church-goers.[(47)]

---

46 For the important role of gambling in the working-class life of this time see Ross McKibbin, 'Working-Class Gambling in Britain 1880-1939,' *Past & Present*, 82 (1979), pp 147-178; Carl Chinn, *Better Betting with a Decent Feller* (Brighton 1991).

47 McLeod, 'New Perspectives,' p 37.

Other working class institutions, such as friendly societies, co-ops, trade unions and radical political organisations, had a more ambivalent relationship with the churches and chapels. Certainly there was no direct conflict involved, and many people did combine membership of religious organisations with membership of such other organisations. On the other hand, there was a potential for rivalry, especially in times of acute social tension. In particular when independent working class politics came to the fore, as in the Chartist period of the 1830s and '40s, and then in the period from the 1880s to the First World War, with the growth of Socialism. Conflicts between independent working-class parties and the churches inevitably arose from the fact that the latter were identified with the old political parties. The majority of Anglican clergy supported the Tory or Conservative Party throughout this period; the majority of Nonconformist ministers were Whigs, Radicals or Liberals; the Roman Catholic clergy were less closely identified with any particular party, but the papal encyclical of 1891, *Rerum Novarum* explicitly condemned Socialism.(48)

---

48 For the Chartist period, see H.U. Faulkner, *Chartism and the Churches* (New York 1916); for the voting record of ministers of religion in the early/mid-Victorian period, John Vincent, *Pollbooks: How Victorians Voted* (Cambridge 1967); for the later period there are many studies at national level, such as David Bebbington, *The Nonconformist Conscience* (London 1982) and G.I.T. Machin, *Politics and the Churches in Great Britain 1869-1921* (Oxford 1987): two useful local studies are Rosemary Chadwick, 'Church and People in Bradford and District 1880-1914: The Protestant Churches in an Urban Industrial Environment,' (University of Oxford Ph.D. thesis 1986), pp 304-339; and Steven Fielding, 'The Irish Catholics of Manchester and Salford: Aspects of their Religious and Political History,' (University of Warwick Ph.D. thesis 1988).

Even in the 1860s and '70s, when most politically active working men supported the Liberal Party, many of them were secularists, standing in self-conscious opposition to the strong element of middle-class Nonconformists in the Party. In this period, the most famous atheist of the nineteenth century, Charles Bradlaugh, won a nation-wide following for his National Secular Society. He combined his atheism with support for a wide range of radical causes, including republicanism, birth control, land reform, and Irish nationalism. In 1880 he was elected Liberal M.P. for Northampton, and his subsequent expulsion form the House of Commons, followed by a long, and ultimately successful campaign to take his seat, turned him into a popular hero.(49)

III

One might well have concluded by now that the case for interpreting Victorian working-class life in secular terms is overwhelmingly strong. Yet as I indicated in the first part of this paper, by no means all historians would accept this conclusion. Their scepticism arises partly from the discovery of new forms of evidence, and partly from the re-evaluation of facts that were already familiar, but which had previously been regarded as relatively unimportant.

---

49 See Edward Royle, *Radicals, Secularists and Republicans: Popular Freethought in Britain 1866-1915* (Manchester 1980).

For instance, it is well known that working-class women were more often involved than working-class men in church or chapel. Most Victorian observers (and most historians), working within a framework of patriarchal assumptions, saw the views of the men as being more important than those of their wives. However, Cox has argued that the reverse was true: since, in working-class households, women took most decisions relating to the home and family, female religiosity had more influence on the rising generation than male indifference.(50) In any case, the growing interest in women's history in recent years has meant that the religious experiences, beliefs and practices of women are increasingly being explored by historians as important subjects in their own right.(51) To take a second example: it has long been known that certain religious denominations, notably the Roman Catholics and the Primitive Methodists, had a large proportion of working-class members, but there has been a strong tendency to play down the significance of this fact on the grounds that the Catholics were mainly Irish immigrants and their descendants, and therefore peripheral to discussion of the *English* working class, and that the Primitive Methodists were not sufficiently numerous to be worth serious consideration. On the other hand, increasing interest by historians in recent years in ethnicity, and in divisions within the English working class, has led to greater interest in Irish Catho-

---

50 Cox, op.cit., pp 34-5.

51 See for instance, the collection editied by Gail Malmgreen, *Religion in the Lives of Englishwomen 1750-1930* (London 1985), and Deborah Valenze, *Sons and Daughters of Prophecy* (Princeton 1985).

lics;[52] and the proliferation of local studies has demonstrated that although national membership of Primitive Methodism was relatively low, they were very important in certain localities, such as the Durham coal-fields.[53]

The *new* evidence on working-class religion has been of two kinds: the first is very specific, but also very difficult to dispute, namely a growing body of statistical evidence on the occupational composition of Nonconformist chapels. The second is much more wide-ranging, but also more difficult to interpret, namely the evidence of oral history.

In recent years there have been several studies which have undertaken the laborious task of taking church membership lists and identifying the members in the

---

52 See the two volumes edited by Roger Swift and Sheridan Gilley, *The Irish in the Victorian City* (London 1985), and *The Irish in Britain 1815-1939* (London 1989). The former volume includes excellent essays on Catholicism by Raphael Samuel, Gerard Connolly and Sheridan Gilley.

53 See Robert Moore, *Pitmen, Politics and Preachers* (London 1974); Robert Colls, *The Pitmen of the Northern Coalfield* (Manchester 1987). Other local studies which highlight the appeal of Primitive Methodism in strongly working-class communities include Barrie Trinder, *The Industrial Revolution in Shropshire* (Chichester 1973), and Eric Hopkins, 'Religious Dissent in Black Country Industrial Villages in the first Half of the Nineteenth Century,' *Journal of Ecclesiastical History*, 34 (1983), pp 411-424. The strength of Primitive Methodism among agricultural labourers in certain regions is well-known: the main studies are Obelkevich, op.cit.; Nigel Scotland, *Methodism and the Revolt of the Field* (Gloucester 1981); Alun Howkins, *Poor Labouring Men: Rural Radicalism in Norfolk 1870-1923* (London 1985).

manuscript census schedules, and many more which have analysed baptismal or marriage registers, in which the occupations of those involved are often listed. All such studies have concluded that most Nonconformist chapels had a substantial working-class element among their members. Gilbert's analysis of Nonconformist baptismal and burial records, mainly from the period 1800-37, suggested that artisans were by far the largest occupational group, and that these, together with smaller numbers of labourers and miners, made up about 75% of the Methodists, Baptists and Congregationalists whose occupations are recorded in the registers. Admittedly the frequent vagueness of occupational descriptions sometimes makes it hard to distinguish between employer, employee and the self-employed. But Gilbert concluded that the great expansion of English Nonconformity between about 1780 and 1840 was mainly due to recruitment among the working class, though he suggested that the chapels were becoming more middle class by the mid-nineteenth century.[54] However, a comprehensive review by Field of local studies of Methodist membership suggests that the pattern described by Gilbert lasted much longer, and that it is only in the twentieth century that Methodism has become predominantly middle class.[55] Phillips analysed records of marriages and baptisms in Nonconformist chapels in Lancashire cotton towns

---

54 Gilbert, op.cit., pp 59-68, 145-9.

55 Clive Field, 'The Social Structure of English Methodism, Eighteenth-Twentieth Centuries,' *British Journal of Sociology*, 28 (1977), pp 199-225; see also K.D.M. Snell, *Church and Chapel in the North Midlands: Religious Observance in the Nineteenth Century* (Leicester 1991), pp 39-45.

between 1830 and 1870. Most showed a preponderance of working-class occupations; even in Bolton's leading Unitarian chapel there was a substantial working-class minority.[56] Membership lists are harder to find. But Bartlett showed that the members of a Bermondsey Baptist chapel in the 1880s were two-thirds working class, and Smith analysed the membership of various chapels in and around Oldham in the 1850s and '60s, and found that most had a predominantly working-class membership, including a large element of factory workers.[57] The most thorough study of this kind has been undertaken by Rosemary Chadwick in respect of Bradford chapels in the 1880s. She found that chapels tended to include considerable numbers of working-class women and of working men in skilled occupations, but that there was an under-representation of men in semi-skilled or unskilled occupations.[58] So it seems likely that chapel membership *was* socially skewed, but that to speak simply of the absence of the working class is an over-simplification.

Elizabeth Roberts concluded from her oral history of the working class in Barrow and Lancaster between 1890 and 1930 that: 'The most striking and obvious fact about religion during the first part of this period is the signifi-

---

56 Paul T. Phillips, *The Sectarian Spirit: Sectarianism, Society and Politics in Victorian Cotton Towns* (Toronto 1982).

57 Bartlett, op.cit., pp 401-3; Mark Smith, 'Religion in Industrial Society: Oldham and Saddleworth 1780-1865,' (University of Oxford D.Phil. thesis 1987), ch 4-5.

58 Chadwick, op.cit., pp 160-1.

cant part it played in all but one family's life.'[59] Oral history evidence has also led me to modify my own views - persuading me that the church-going minority in the Victorian working class was larger than has previously been realised, that the decline of the churches was more gradual than historians have generally assumed, and that the influence of the churches and chapels on non-church-going working-class people was greater than has usually been suggested. So in what ways has oral evidence undermined existing orthodoxies?

In the first place it suggests that the proportion of working-class people who went to church or chapel with some degree of frequency is rather higher than anyone might have guessed.[60] Thompson and Vigne interviewed about 500 people born between 1872 and 1908 from selected regions of Britain about their memories of the period before 1918. Taking all the interviews with people brought up in working-class families in industrial regions of England, about 40% of interviewees claimed that their mother attended church or chapel with some degree of frequency in their childhood - though the figure for London (22%) was far below average. In London, the north Midlands, the Potteries and the north-east the figure for fathers was around 20%, but it was higher in Lancashire (32%) and Yorkshire (40%). The average for both sexes is thus around 30% - which is somewhat higher than censuses taken on a single Sunday might suggest. (See Appen-

---

59 Elizabeth Roberts, *Working Class Barrow and Lancaster 1890-1930* (Lancaster 1976), p 62.

60 McLeod, 'New Perspectives,' p 33.

dix.) The probable explanation is that because of illness, tiredness or child-care problems, working-class church-goers were less likely than their middle-class counterparts to attend every week, and that counts like that taken nationally on 30 March 1851 accordingly under-represented the extent of working-class attendance.

A second point is that the oral evidence provides graphic illustration of the arguments by Ainsworth and Cox, quoted earlier, that the churches had a pervasive social influence even in communities where church-going was low. Many poor families came to depend on the free breakfasts and other benefits and treats provided by churches and chapels. A Preston woman, born in 1898 of poor Catholic parents, remembers attending one of the local Protestant missions nearly every week. Her earliest happy memory was of the free breakfasts at Shepherd Street mission, which 'used to be a grand place for people who were very poor. ...Mr Williams never sent anyone away.' She also enjoyed lantern shows at the Band of Hope, and she went to an Anglican mission, where she paid a penny or two a week, and ended up with a trip to Southport. Churches and chapels were social centres for wide sections of the population, providing in one way or another for both sexes and all age-groups. 'That was the social life of the Island,' said a Barrow interviewee, 'around the church, because there was very little else, no telly, no radio, and people got linked with the church, and they attended all the functions that took place.'[61] Doug Reid has noted that in Birmingham, the churches did not simply follow the lead set by secular bodies, but from

---

61 Ibid., p 35.

the 1850s onwards they often played a pioneering role in extending leisure facilities.[62] An important figure here was the Rev J.C.Miller, vicar of St Martin's in the 1850s, who established a flourishing Working Men's Association. Concerts, excursions and evening classes were all part of the fare, and from about the 1880s, the churches were taking an active part in the craze for cricket, football and boxing. Indeed many of the leading football teams of to-day have their origins in church clubs, notable examples including Aston Villa, Everton and Bolton Wanderers.[63]

The most striking example of the inescapable presence of the church and chapel was the fact that the overwhelming majority of working-class children went to Sunday School. There have been many different views among historians as to the causes and consequences of this. The most widely influential version was that propounded thirty years ago by E.P.Thompson in his classic account of the period before 1832: he stressed the indoctrination and 'religious terrorism' practised in the Sunday Schools, and saw them as an effective means of training a new generation of docile factory hands.[64] Since then, historians of the Victorian period have advanced at least four other interpretations. Laqueur agreed that Sun-

---

62 Douglas A. Reid, 'Labour, Leisure and Politics in Birmingham c.1800-1875,' (University of Birmingham Ph.D. thesis 1985).

63 Tony Mason, *Association Football and English Society 1863-1915* (Brighton 1980), pp 24-26.

64 E.P. Thompson, *The Making of the English Working Class* (2nd edition, Harmondsworth 1968), pp 412-416.

day Schools were effective, but he presented a much more sympathetic picture of their objectives and methods, and he stressed their popularity both with working-class parents and with many of the children;[65] Roberts also saw Sunday Schools as popular, though principally because of the treats they provided;[66] Humphries thought the children resented going to Sunday School, and did their best to disrupt the classes;[67] and Cox argued that, while enjoyably chaotic from the children's point of view, the schools were ineffective as a means of inculcating religion, or anything else.[68] These very wide differences of interpretation partly arise, no doubt, from the different ideological presuppositions of the historians.

But the divergence probably also arises from the very varied character of an institution, which was sponsored by many very different religious denominations in social environments of many different kinds, which evolved over time, and which inevitably evoked many different kinds of individual response on the part of the millions of children who experienced it. Nonetheless, one generalisation that can be made is that the almost universal

---

65 Thomas Walter Laqueur, *Religion and Respectability: Sunday Schools and Working Class Culture 1780-1850* (New Haven 1976), ch 6-7.

66 Roberts, *Working Class Barrow and Lancaster*, pp 62-4, 68.

67 Stephen Humphries, *Hooligans or Rebels? An Oral History of Working-Class Childhood and Youth 1889-1939* (Oxford 1981), pp 130-134.

68 Cox, op.cit., pp 95-6, 227-8.

exposure of Victorian working-class children to the Sunday School meant that the great majority of the population grew up with a basic acquaintance with the Bible, Christian hymns and Christian doctrine. For many people, this acquaintance remained basic, and the resulting sense of Christian identity was largely passive; but the achievement of the Sunday Schools, later assisted by the various kinds of day school, was to establish some form of Christian belief as being normal. It required a conscious act of will, accompanied perhaps by some sense of an uncomfortable heroism, to join the 'infidels' in rejecting this belief[(69)] - though clergymen were all too conscious of the fact that it was not easy to change this largely passive religion into some more active form of Christian commitment.

Most important of all, the oral evidence highlights aspects of religious belief and practice that are otherwise hidden from public view. It is clear from this that outside observers were much too ready to assume that those who seldom or never went to church were 'secular' or 'indifferent' in their religious outlook. There were indeed people who could be fairly described in such terms. But there were also a good many people whose religious views were much more complex. There were for instance many non-church-goers who prayed, read the Bible, or sang hymns, or had strongly held ideas on Christian ethics. Hymns, in particular, were sung in many places beside churches and schools. Probably no kind of music

---

69 Susan Budd, *Varieties of Unbelief: Atheists and Agnostics in English Society 1850-1960* (London 1977), p 110, discusses the psychological barriers to unbelief and the sense of being an outsider that secularists suffered.

was so universally familiar in England during the nineteenth and early twentieth centuries, and there were many different kinds of situation which lent themselves to hymn-singing.[70] In the earlier part of the nineteenth century, women workers in the Yorkshire woollen industry were said to alternate between gossiping and singing hymns as they worked in the burling shed; in the years around the end of the century Sunday evening singing hymns around the piano was an established ritual in many working-class, as well as middle-class families; soldiers at the front in World War I would keep their spirits up by singing hymns, sometimes introducing bawdy alternatives to the official words.[71] A woman brought up around the turn of the century in the dockland borough of Bermondsey remembers her mother singing hymns as she worked on her sewing machine; and a Barrow woman remembers her non-church-going father returning from Saturday night drinking bouts to sit on the toilet singing all Sunday's hymns.[72] There is a similar scene in *The Ragged Trousered Philanthropists*, where the workers are feeling in a mellow frame of mind on the way back

---

70 Jim Obelkevich, 'Music and Religion in the Nineteenth Century,' Jim Obelkevich, Lyndal Roper and Raphael Samuel (eds.), *Disciplines of Faith* (London 1987), p 554. See also Lionel Adey, *Class and Idol in the English Hymn* (Vancouver 1988).

71 J. Lawson, *Letters to the Young on Progress in Pudsey during the last Sixty Years* (Stanningley 1887), pp 33-34; Obelkevich, 'Music and Religion,' loc.cit.; Alan Wilkinson, *The Church of England and the First World War* (London 1978), pp 156-158.

72 Interviews on Family Life and Work Experience, no 235, p 12; Elizabeth Roberts, Interview with Mrs S2B, p 16 (Centre for North-West Regional Studies, University of Lancaster).

from the firm' s annual beano, and pass the journey in singing the choruses of such Moody and Sankey favourites as 'Pull for the Shore' and 'Where is my Wandering Boy?'[73] Hymns could express emotions of joy and of sorrow, of gratitude or of defiance, of hope or of longing, in an idiom that was acceptable to all but the relatively few convinced secularists. They often had great nostalgic appeal for those who had become estranged from the church or had lost their religious faith. In church and home they could be used to establish an emotional unity which might at least temporarily cover over internal divisions. Prayer, too, had a role in the day to day life of many non-church-going families - though by its nature it was more likely than hymn-singing to be a private matter. About half the working-class Londoners interviewed by Thompson and Vigne revealed that they had been taught prayers by their mother. One woman whose mother did *not* say prayers with her saw this as a reflection of her mother's harsh and insensitive nature - that time together at the bedside was a moment of special intimacy, and she made sure that *her* children were taught their prayers. From other interviews, and from working-class autobiographies, we have accounts of working-class women praying at the bedside of sick neighbours, or with bereaved relatives, praying for money when they had run out of food, or praying for strength in times of special stress.[74] Praying in public seems to

---

73 Tressell, op.cit., p 493.

74 Raphael Samuel, East End MS, interview with Mrs Prentice, p 36; Kathleen Woodward, *Jipping Street* (London 1928), p 131; Dolly Scannell, *Mother Knew Best* (London 1975), p 16; McLeod, 'New Perspectives,' pp 37-8.

have been mainly a female activity in working-class households, though sometimes we have accounts of men praying privately - for instance, before going into battle in World War I.[75]

One other important area of working-class life has always been problematic so far as the secular interpretation is concerned, namely politics. In the 1830s and '4Os, Chartists who were disillusioned with the mainstream churches and chapels, formed Chartist Churches - which may reflect anti-clericalism, but scarcely suggests a secular outlook.[76] In the mid-Victorian years, when the Liberals and Conservatives held the loyalty of most working-class voters, it is well-established that sectarian loyalty had a major influence on the choice that working-class voters made.[77] With the revival of socialist and independent labour politics at the end of the nineteenth century, it is clear that a high proportion of labour activists were drawn from a church and chapel background, and that many of them articulated their Socialism in Christian terms.[78] Again, the formation from

---

75 David S. Cairns (ed.), *The Army and Religion* (London 1919), p 9.

76 See Faulkner, op.cit..

77 Joyce, op.cit., pp 242-3. A statistical study suggests that religious factors were a decisive influence on voting right up to 1914: Kenneth D. Wald, *Crosses on the Ballot* (Princeton 1983).

78 Hugh McLeod, 'Religion in the British and German Labour Movements c. 1890-1914: A Comparison,' *Bulletin of the Society for the Study of Labour History*, 50 (1986), pp 25-35 provides an overview. More detailed local studies include Ainsworth, op.cit., (Lancashire) and Moore, op.cit., (Durham).

1891 onwards of Labour Churches reflected the fact that many socialist activists who had become disillusioned with the mainstream churches still wanted to affirm the religious basis of the labour cause.[79] Of course, it could well be argued that many working-class people were only intermittently interested in politics, and some not at all, and that the spread of trade unionism in the pre-World War I period was very uneven, with many industries being little affected. Nonetheless the minority of the working class which was strongly active in politics and trade unionism cannot be as sharply separated from the less committed majority as this argument might suggest. There were periods, for instance at the peak of Chartism in the later 1830s and early 1840s, or during the 'Great Labour Unrest' immediately before World War I, when political awareness was at a much higher level than at other times, and there were more localised upsurges of political enthusiasm like that in Bradford in the early 1890s which resulted in the formation of the Independent Labour Party. Actions and attitudes during these crisis periods provide important pointers to underlying attitudes which may be partly submerged at other times. The role of religion in working-class politics was complex and many-sided, but it was in many ways important. I shall sum it up under the headings of personnel, rhetoric, and sectarian identity.

So far as rhetoric is concerned, many historians have demonstrated the importance of Christian concepts and

---

79 The definitive study is D.F. Summers, 'The Labour Church and Allied Movements of the late Nineteenth and early Twnetieth Centuries,' (University of Edinburgh Ph.D. thesis 1958). There is a useful introduction in Inglis, op.cit..

biblical language for the presentation of the Chartist, Labour or socialist message. Eileen Yeo has shown how Christianity was in the 1830s and '40s contested territory : Whigs, Tories and Chartists all tried to prove that the Bible when properly understood supported their own case. Thus Chartist demands were legitimated by reference to the Bible; biblical language was used to enhance the appeal of the Chartist vision of the future; and divine help was invoked in order to withstand the rigours of the struggle.[80] With the rise of socialism from the 1880s, a similar biblical rhetoric was used by such popular speakers as George Lansbury in London or Philip Snowden in Lancashire and Yorkshire, as well as by the most charismatic of all the socialists of his generation, the Scottish Keir Hardie.[81]

The use of Christian language could also affect in more profound ways the Chartist or socialist understanding of their message. Politics were understood in ethical terms, and recruits to the cause were seen as converts. A characteristic expression of this way of thinking was the 'ethical socialism' of the years around 1900, which emphasised 'the brotherhood of man' rather than 'the class struggle', which tended to be pacifist, and was often

---

80 Eileen Yeo, op.cit; see also her paper on 'Chartist Religious Belief and the Theology of Liberation,' in Obelkevich, Roper and Samuel (eds.), op.cit., pp 410-421.

81 See Gillian Rose, 'Locality, Politics and Culture: Poplar in the 1920s' (University of London Ph.D. thesis 1989), pp 278-80, which discusses the relationship between Lansbury's politics and religion; Keith Laybourn and David James (eds.), *Philip Snowden* (Bradford 1987); K.O. Morgan, *Keir Hardie* (London 1975).

highly moralistic.[82]

So far as personnel is concerned the striking point is the frequency with which men from a strongly religious background were elected to positions of responsibility in the labour movement. This phenomenon is best documented in the case of the mining and agricultural trade unions. The north-east offers an interesting example: church-going was rather low in the mining districts of Durham and Northumberland, and it is likely that most miners were not themselves active Methodists. Yet they repeatedly elected Methodists to union office and to posts as checkweighmen.[83] When they got together in the pub, miners might have a bit of a laugh at the expense of their more straight-laced Methodist colleague, but when it came to choosing someone who could be entrusted with branch funds, or who would speak out on their behalf in a dispute, it was very often the Methodist who got their vote. A study of the religious background of 249 Labour M.P.s in the 1929-31 Parliament showed that 105 claimed to be Nonconformists, whereas only 8 said they were atheists or agnostics. While no doubt there were many whose religious affiliation was fairly nominal, there were also a considerable number whose whole political outlook had been moulded by their religion. Here for instance are

---

82 See Stephen Yeo, 'A New Life: The Religion of Socialism in Britain 1883-96,' *History Workshop Journal*, 4 (1977), pp 5-56; and for a critique of this form of socialism, William Knox, 'Religion and the Scottish Labour Movement,' *Journal of Contemporary History*, 23, (1988), pp 609-630.

83 Moore, op.cit; see also, for discussion of this phenomenon, E.J. Hobsbawm, *Primitive Rebels* (2nd edition, Manchester 1970).

the comments by George Lansbury, the East End M.P., who led the Party in the early 30s:

> Religion is not a matter for Sunday and Monday but for whole life. Education cannot be carried on apart from religion. Anything in industry or politics that conflicts with our Lord's teaching must be removed, and men and women must be given opportunity so to live that they express in their daily life the law of love. We Labour believe that it is a denial of our Lord's teaching that we fight each other for our daily bread. In fact we believe that it is that personal struggle to get above each other which causes most of the evil in the world, and consequently we are always working to substitute in place of that struggle co-operation.(84)

Sectarian identity was particularly important in the years of Liberal and Conservative hegemony. Whereas Chartists and socialists tried to attract the support of working men, irrespective of denominational affiliation (not always with complete success), sectarianism was fundamental to the appeal of Liberalism and Conservatism. The Conservatives presented themselves in Lancashire as the Protestant Party, arrayed against the forces of Irish immigrant Catholicism.(85) Elsewhere, they were associated with the Church of England in its battles against

---

84 Franz Linden, *Sozialismus und Religion* (Leipzig 1932), pp 110-111, 155.

85 See P.J. Waller, *Democracy and Sectarianism: A Social and Political History of Liverpool 1868-1939* (Liverpool 1981).

Nonconformity. The Liberals championed the rights and interests of religious minorities. They were linked especially closely with the Nonconformist chapels. But they also attracted support from Roman Catholics, Jews and Secularists.[86] One interesting statistic that illustrates the importance of the sectarian factor is provided by the Thompson-Vigne interviews. Taking interviews with those brought up in working-class families in industrial districts of Britain, other than Lancashire, we find that 64% of non-church-going fathers with children at an Anglican Sunday School voted Tory, but only 25% of non-church-going fathers with children at a Nonconformist Sunday School; in Lancashire, 67% of Protestant fathers whose voting habits are known voted Tory, but only 7% of Roman Catholic fathers did so. The conclusion to be drawn is that sectarian identity was a reality for many people whose attachment to their church or chapel was actually fairly loose.[87] This was most obviously so in Lancashire, where the deep divide between Protestant and Catholic affected where people lived and where they worked. Young people were strongly discouraged from finding marriage partners of the wrong faith, and in towns like Liverpool and Preston, a huge

---

86 Bebbington, op.cit.; Fielding, op.cit.; Royle, op.cit.; Geoffrey Alderman, *The Jewish Community in British Politics* (Oxford 1983). The Jewish voting pattern was particularly complex: heavily Liberal until the 1880s, the Jewish vote then diversified as many of the middle class moved to Liberal Unionism or Conservatism, while Socialism gained ground among working-class immigrants. However, the 1906 election (following the Conservative Aliens Act) saw a last revival of Jewish Liberalism.

87 McLeod, 'New Perspectives,' p 36.

folk-lore developed about the supposed qualities of the other community. Comments made in passing often reveal a lot about popular attitudes: a Barrow woman who had worked in a convent remarked that the nuns were very clean, 'although they were Catholics'; a Preston woman noted that her mother always went to a 'Catholic doctor'.[(88)] But the divide between church and chapel was important too. Again, it could have repercussions on where people worked, as some employers preferred to take on workers of their own denomination. But church and chapel also came to be associated with distinctive life-styles. Chapel-goers saw themselves as down-to-earth people, with a simple and sincere faith, and a horror of any kind of grovelling before social 'superiors'. Church people dismissed Nonconformists as narrow-minded Puritans; they were proud of their own more relaxed attitude to life, and they also were proud of their patriotism - only an Anglican could be one hundred per-cent English, and John Bull was a typical Anglican.[(89)]

IV

Is it possible to reconcile such a diversity of interpretations? First, it has to be recognised that all types of sources contain their inherent biases. For instance, the large body of commentary on working-class life by middle-

---

88 Ibid., pp 42-3.

89 Ibid., p 43; Joyce, op.cit., pp 173-8, 187-91; Wald, op.cit., ch 7.

class observers is limited in value both by the fact that the comments are those of outsiders and by the fact that these observers very often were looking for evidence in support of their own programmes of religious or political action. It is extraordinary, for instance, how willing historians have often been to take Friedrich Engels' views on working-class religion at face-value.[90] If Engels' assertions need to be treated with some degree of caution, this rule applies equally to the many accounts of their parishes, both favourable and hostile, that were written by clergymen. Autobiographies and oral history are potentially an invaluable means of enabling working-class people to speak for themselves; but here too, there are major problems of interpretation, not least because of the general human tendencies towards nostalgia, self-justification, and the reinterpretation of experience in the light of intervening events. It should also be noted that the selection of and presentation of events by autobiographers is considerably influenced by the desire to tell a good story.[91] All of this may well be stating the obvious, but it is worth mentioning because the extreme divergence between the views of different historians studying the same subject is often caused by dependence on different sources and by the tendency to use these sources in an uncritical way.

---

90 For which, see F. Engels, *The Condition of the Working Class in England* (English translation, Oxford 1958), p 141.

91 For discussion of the use of such sources see David Vincent, *Bread, Knowledge and Freedom: A Study of Nineteenth-Century Working Class Autobiography* (London 1981); Paul Thompson, *The Voice of the Past: Oral History* (Oxford 1978).

The divergence between historians' interpretations of nineteenth-century working-class religion is also partly explicable in terms of the diversity of the Victorian working class. There undoubtedly were important religious differences between regions, between ethnic groups, between occupational groups, and between men and women. And, as was mentioned earlier, there were changes over time, though historians are not agreed as to exactly how and when these happened.

The big regional variations both in the total level and the denominational distribution of church-going were indicated by the 1851 national religious census and by the local censuses conducted in the later part of the century.[(92)] By the 1880s, there was a considerable degree of residential segregation in the larger towns, so it is possible to break down the census results in order to compare church-going in working-class and in middle-class districts. These breakdowns show that, although middle-class church-going was nearly always higher than working-class church-going, both the middle-class and the working-class patterns varied by region.(See Appendix.) Going back to 1851 it is evident that there was a clear regional pattern of church-going which was most strongly marked in rural areas, but which was reflected in the towns as as well. There was a belt of high church-

---

92 Hugh McLeod, 'Class, Community and Region: The Religious Geography of Nineteenth-Century England,' M. Hill (ed.), *A Sociological Yearbook of Religion in Britain, 6* (London 1973), pp 29-72; Hugh McLeod, 'Religion,' John Langton and R.J. Morris (eds.), *Atlas of Industrializing Britain 1780-1914* (London 1986), pp 212-217.

going, stretching from the south-west through the south and east midlands to East Anglia; the north Midlands, Yorkshire and Kent were around average; and there were areas of low attendance in Middlesex, Surrey and Sussex, in the west Midlands, Lancashire and Cumbria and the north-east. So far as denominational affiliations were concerned, Anglicanism was predominant south of the Trent, though the Nonconformists had strongholds in Cornwall and parts of the east Midlands and East Anglia. North of the Trent, the Pennines, and the land to the east, were Nonconformist territory; west of the Pennines, Anglicanism predominated, though with local pockets of Roman Catholic strength, especially in Lancashire. Those industrial districts with high levels of church-going were usually strongholds of Nonconformity - for instance the Cornish mining areas, the West Country woollen district, the Northamptonshire shoe- making belt, the nail-making areas of the Black Country, the weaving districts of north-east Lancashire. The censuses of the 1880s and '90s showed that there quite wide variations in church-going levels even between large towns. Among those surveyed, Bristol came top with an attendance rate of 53% and Birmingham bottom with 23%. Also in the top group (with attendance rates of over 40%) was Hull. In the bottom group (with rates under 30%) were London, Sheffield and the Potteries. In the middle, with rates bunched around 33% were Liverpool, Bradford, Nottingham, Bolton and Portsmouth.(See Appendix.)

A crucial dividing line is that of gender.[(93)] In all areas

---

93 In this paragraph I am drawing on material from ch 7 of Hugh McLeod, *Poverty and Piety: Working-Class Religion in Berlin, London and New York 1870-1914* (forthcoming, from Holmes & Meier,

of Victorian society, women were more likely than men to be actively involved in a church or chapel; conversely, men were far more likely than women to join a secularist organisation, and more men than women were agnostics. It was in working-class areas that the difference in church membership and attendance patterns was most marked.[94] Admittedly the gulf was widest in regions like the north-east dominated by mining and heavy engineering, where few women had jobs, and there was a sharp divide between the home-based culture of working-class women and the male culture based on the workplace and on pubs and clubs. It was narrower in areas like Lancashire where many women worked in textile factories, and there was more overlap between male and female roles - men were more likely to help in the home, and they might take on tasks, like taking the children to church, which in other parts of the country fell within the female sphere. So the patterns of male and female religiosity were not exactly the same from one part of the country to another. But, as a general rule, there was a whole series of factors which tended to give religious organisations and religion generally a bigger role in the lives of working-class women than of

---

New York). The fullest discussion of this theme is in Valenze, op.cit. There are useful briefer discussions in Chadwick, op.cit., pp 171-3, and Rose, op.cit., pp 264-9. In Scotland valuable work on the religion of working-class women has been done by Jayne Stephenson and Callum Brown: see their article, 'Sprouting Wings? Women and Religion in Scotland c.1890-c.1950,' E. Gordon and E. Breitenbach (eds.), *Out of Bounds: Women in Scotland in the 19th and 20th Centuries*, forthcoming from Edinburgh University Press.

94 Chadwick, op.cit., p 163.

working-class men. One important consideration was that churches and chapels provided the one sphere outside the home where women were welcomed, where they could enjoy some degree of responsibility, and where they could relax with other women. Particularly important, in this respect, were the mothers' meetings, which usually met on Monday afternoon or evening, combining hymn-singing and some kind of religious chat with a certain amount of socialising, and the purchase of materials at low prices. They flourished in London in the later nineteenth century, and attracted many poor women who seldom got out of the house at other times.[95] On the other hand, the lives of working-class men were much less restricted, and churches and chapels had to compete with many other institutions, most notably the pubs. Religion also impinged in many ways on the home sphere, which was especially the concern of women: the proper upbringing of children began with ensuring that they were baptised; as they got older, it meant that they needed to know the difference between right and wrong - this certainly required that they went to Sunday School, and in many families it included learning something about God and praying every night. All these things fell within the mother's sphere of responsibility - though fathers sometimes added their bit by saying grace before meals, or - in more strongly devout families - reading the Bible to the family at night. Sexual stereotyping also played a role in the divergence between male and female religious habits which appeared during the teenage years:

95 Frank Prochaska, 'A Mother's Country: Mothers' Meetings and Family Welfare in Britain 1850-1950,' *History*, 74 (1989), pp 379-399.

overt religiosity seemed to fit less well with the 'male' qualities of strength and aggression than with the 'female' qualities of sensitivity and compassion. Teenage girls who were known to be devout were likely to receive the approval of parents and workmates; boys who were strongly religious might have to undergo a certain amount of ridicule. This was the reason for the Victorian craze for 'muscular Christianity', initiated by Charles Kingsley and Thomas Hughes in the later 1850s, with a public school audience in mind, and later adopted by many vicars of working-class parishes who formed football clubs and instructed members of their boys' club in boxing, in order to refute claims that Christianity was 'feminine'. In the late Victorian and Edwardian periods, similar ideas also gave rise to a plethora of uniformed organisations, like the Scouts and the Boys Brigade, which combined religion with militarism and imperialism.[(96)]

The ethnic dimension of Victorian working-class history is also important, and this too of course was closely bound up with religion. The largest ethnic minority were the Irish, who were moving into the cities and industrial districts of England throughout the nineteenth century, but most notably in the 1840s and '50s, following the disastrous famine. Throughout the Victorian period there were large Irish districts in London, Liverpool and Manchester, and a major Irish presence in most

---

96 Norman Vance, *Sinews of the Spirit* (Cambridge 1985); John Spinghall, 'Building Character in the British Boy: The Attempt to extend Christian Manliness to Working-Class Adolsecents, 1880-1914,' J.A. Mangan and James Walvin (eds.), *Manliness and Morality: Middle-Class Masculinity in Britain and America 1800-1940* (Manchester 1987), pp 52-74.

of the country s industrial districts, most notably in Lancashire. There was a more localised immigration of Jews from eastern Europe, concentrated mainly on the period 1881-1905, which transformed certain districts of London, Manchester and Leeds.[97]

This meant that in areas like Liverpool's Scotland Road or London's Whitechapel there were large and compact communities with religious cultures very different from those of the Protestant working class. So far as the Irish Catholics were concerned, one important aspect if this was the central role of the 'fathers' and the 'sisters'. Another was the vital part played in their religious life by the saints, and especially the Blessed Virgin Mary, images of whom stood in churches, were stamped onto the medallions worn by her devotees, and hung on the walls of Catholic homes. It was a highly visual religious culture in which processions through the streets and giant church buildings, towering over the terraces of two-storey cottages, played an essential part and where, on the occasion of important Marian festivals, banners hanging across the street would declare 'Hail, Queen of Heaven' or 'God bless our Pope'. It was also a culture keenly attuned to the miraculous, where particularly holy priests were credited with healing powers, and where in the early twentieth century Lourdes became a topic of

---

97 The standard account is Lloyd P. Gartner, *The Jewish Immigrant in Britain 1870-1914* (2nd edition, London, 1973); an outstanding recent study is David Feldman, 'Immigrants and Workers, Englishmen and Jews: Jewish Immigrants to the East End of London 1880-1906,' (University of Cambridge Ph.D. thesis 1985).

consuming interest.[98] All this was far removed from the more pragmatic and low-key style of native Protestantism, where all forms of religion were assessed in terms of their practical consequences, and Irish Catholicism was found wanting because of the alleged propensity of its devotees for heavy drinking.[99]

Differences of income and status within the working class clearly had repercussions for religion too. Both Anglican and Nonconformist church attendance was higher in upper working-class districts than in poorer areas, and there is some evidence to suggest that the same was true for Catholics.[100] In fact some contemporaries suggested that the differences in culture and life-style between the very poor and the respectable working class were as great as those between the latter and the middle class. For instance, in the north-west London district of Queens

---

98 See, for instance, Gerard Connolly, '"Little Brother be at Peace": The Priest as Holy Man in the Nineteenth century Ghetto,' W.J. Sheils (ed.), *The Church and Healing*, Studies in Church History 19, (Oxford 1982), pp 191-206; Sheridan Gilley, 'The Catholic Faith of the Irish Slums,' Dyos and Wolff (eds.), op.cit., 2, pp 837-853; Bartlett, op.cit., pp 302-14; Fielding, op.cit., pp 94-98.

99 See the characteristic comment by Charles Booth that the London Irish were 'as a rule devout ... but at the same time they are great beggars, as well as heavy drinkers, and there is no sign that the form that practical religion takes in their case helps to make them in these respects either more self-reliant or more self-restrained'. Booth, op.cit., 3rd series, 7, p 401.

100 Hugh McLeod, *Class and Religion in the late Victorian City* (London 1974), pp 26-8, 32, 40-1.

Park, with its railway and post office workers, and a flourishing Congregational chapel, Charles Booth claimed that the majority of the population were church-goers: 'The gulf that lies between these people and the cadging poor south of the canal is not easily bridged. Both may be accounted members of the working classes, but how far apart!'[101]

All the dividing-lines so far discussed were quite familiar to contemporaries, and it was well-known that they had a bearing on religious differences. But there was still a tendency to generalise about the 'typical' working man, or to postulate a predominant attitude in terms of which everything else could be regarded as rather eccentric. It may be, however, that we need a more pluralistic conception of working class religious attitudes and behaviour, in which the existence of a wide spectrum of views is recognised. We know quite a lot about those at either extreme - the committed believers and the convinced secularists. But we know much less about those who fell somewhere in between.

My analysis of the Thompson and Vigne interviews with 45 Londoners brought up in working-class homes, suggested that slightly under a third came from a home with a strongly religious ethos, and slightly under a third from a home with an ethos of indifference or hostility to religion, with the remainder of homes falling somewhere between these extremes.[102] In these households, the adults

---

101 Booth, op.cit., 3rd series, 3, pp 142-5.

102 See McLeod, *Poverty and Piety* (forthcoming).

did not attend regular Sunday services at church or chapel, though they might attend a place of worship on special occasions, such as Watch Night, and the mother might attend a mothers' meeting; children were frequently taught their prayers and in many cases grace was said before meals, but there might be a somewhat routine air to these rituals, so that the continual need for God's protection and guidance was less emphasised than in more devout families. They might well have strong views on 'practical Christianity', based, Elizabeth Roberts suggests in her study of working-class women in Lancashire, on a mixture of 'loving your neighbour', the work ethic, a keen sense of justice, and strict sexual taboos.[103] This, I would guess, is what a Poplar man had in mind when he described his parents as 'one hundred per cent Christians, but not church-goers'.[104]

Certainly the activist minorities of committed believers or secularists had an influence out of proportion to their numbers. A large part of history is after all made by activist minorities, and a history which focuses mainly on dramatic changes will need to focus mainly on these activists. But a history which is concerned with how life was experienced by the majority of those living at the time needs to give serious attention to those whose beliefs were less clearly defined and more ambiguous, and

---

103 Roberts, *A Woman's Place*, pp 4-6.

104 Family Life and Work Experience, no 70, p 16.

who maybe had a foot in several camps.[105] Very probably, in most other parts of the country, the proportion of strongly religious families would have been somewhat higher than in London, and the proportion of the hostile or indifferent somewhat lower. But we need to know much more about the large intermediate group, if we are to understand what religion meant to the majority of Victorian working-class people.

---

105 Gerald Parsons in his essay on Victorian working-class religion (op.cit., 2, pp 84-5) reaches rather similar conclusions. Between the extremes of committed religion or irreligion, he stresses the prevalence of 'diffusive Christianity', and argues that with the decline of formal religious attachment by the middle class in the twentieth century, this has become 'the predominant - if still too little recognised - religious style of the majority of the nation as a whole'.

Appendix

Church attendance as a percentage of population as reported in various local censuses conducted by newspapers between 1881 and 1892.

Year	City	Pop. in 000s	CofE	RC	Major NC	Other	Total
1881	Liverpool	552	9.8	11.3	7.9	4.2	33.2
1881	Sheffield	284	10.8	2.1	8.2	8.1	29.2
1881	Bristol	207	21.7	3.1	15.5	13.4	53.7
1881	Bradford	194	8.1	4.6	12.3	6.7	31.7
1881	Portsmouth & Gosport	150	17.3	1.8	9.4	7.6	36.1
1881	Leicester	122	12.9	1.7	15.6	8.3	38.5
1886	London	4,059	13.5	2.8	8.6	3.6	28.5
1892	Birmingham	580	10.0	1.8	7.6	3.5	22.9

District	Social Character	CofE	RC	Major NC	Other	Total
London						
Shoreditch	Poor	7.7	1.9	3.7	1.6	14.9
Battersea	Working class	10.3	1.3	5.9	3.8	21.3
Hackney	Mixed	14.6	1.9	13.5	3.4	33.4
Hampstead	Middle class	26.3	2.0	11.3	1.3	40.9
Birmingham						
St Stephen, St Mary, St Bartholomew	Poor	6.2	2.3	2.5	2.6	13.6
Bordesley & Balsall Heath	Working class	6.7	—	10.2	3.8	20.7
Handsworth	Mixed	16.5	—	13.2	3.9	33.6
Moseley & Kings Heath	Middle class	27.1	—	13.3	0.2	40.6

Sheffield						
North	Poor	5.3	4.7	3.8	0.7	14.5
Attercliffe	Working class	6.9	1.6	8.2	9.0	25.7
Nether Hallam	Mixed	11.6	—	8.3	10.7	30.6
Liverpool						
Exchange & Vauxhall	Catholic working class	2.2	30.7	2.3	1.6	36.8
Kirkdale	Protestant working class	6.4	4.2	10.6	1.4	22.6
Toxteth	Mixed	10.6	7.6	10.2	2.9	31.3
Abercromby	Middle class	22.9	6.2	16.7	11.2	57.0
Bristol						
Bedminster	Working class	14.5	—	7.3	16.0	37.8
St Philip & St Jacob	Working class	12.5	1.7	10.2	16.8	41.2
Clifton & Westbury	Middle class	33.3	6.5	22.2	3.5	65.5
Bradford						
South, North, Bradford Moor	Working class	5.9	0.8	8.3	2.4	17.4
Manningham	Mixed	18.9	—	13.8	4.8	37.5
Portsmouth						
Kingston	Working class	10.6	—	6.3	6.3	23.2
Southsea	Middle class	35.9	—	14.0	0.1	50.0
Leicester						
North & Middle St Margarets	Working class	8.3	1.8	6.9	11.0	28.0
East St Mary & East St Margarets	Middle class	19.2	3.7	34.3	9.2	66.4

'Major NC' comprises the four major Nonconformist denominations of relatively high social status, namely the Congregationalists, Baptists, Wesleyan Methodists and Presbyterians.

'Others' includes all denominations not counted under the other three headings, most notably the Primitive Methodists, Free Methodists, Methodist New Connexion, Brethren and Salvation Army.

Source: Hugh McLeod, 'Class, Community and Region: The Religious Geography of Nineteenth Century England,' M. Hill (ed.), *A Sociological Yearbook of Religion in Britain 6* (London 1973), pp 29-72.

BIBLIOGRAPHIC NOTE

For detailed suggestions, see the footnotes. The major stages in the historiography can be traced by reading the following five books: E.R. Wickham, *Church and People in an Industrial City* (London 1957); K.S. Inglis, *Churches and the Working Classes in Victorian England* (London 1963); Hugh McLeod, *Class and Religion in the late Victorian City* (London 1974); A.D. Gilbert, *Religion and Society in Industrial England: Church, Chapel and Social Change 1740-1914* (London 1976); Jeffrey Cox, *English Churches in a Secular Society: Lambeth 1870-1930* (Oxford 1982). Hugh McLeod, *Religion and the Working Class in Nineteenth Century Britain* (Basingstoke 1984) reviews the state of knowledge at that time and the major debates. Unfortunately most of the major research done since then still remains in unpublished theses.